MATISSE'S GARDEN

Samantha Friedman
Illustrations by Cristina Amodeo

with reproductions of works by Henri Matisse

The Museum of Modern Art, New York

One day the artist Henri Matisse
cut a small bird from a piece of white paper.

It was a simple shape, but he liked the way
it looked and didn't want to throw it out.
So he pinned it on the wall of his apartment
to cover up a stain.

The bird seemed lonely by itself. So Matisse cut
out more shapes, which joined the bird on the wall.

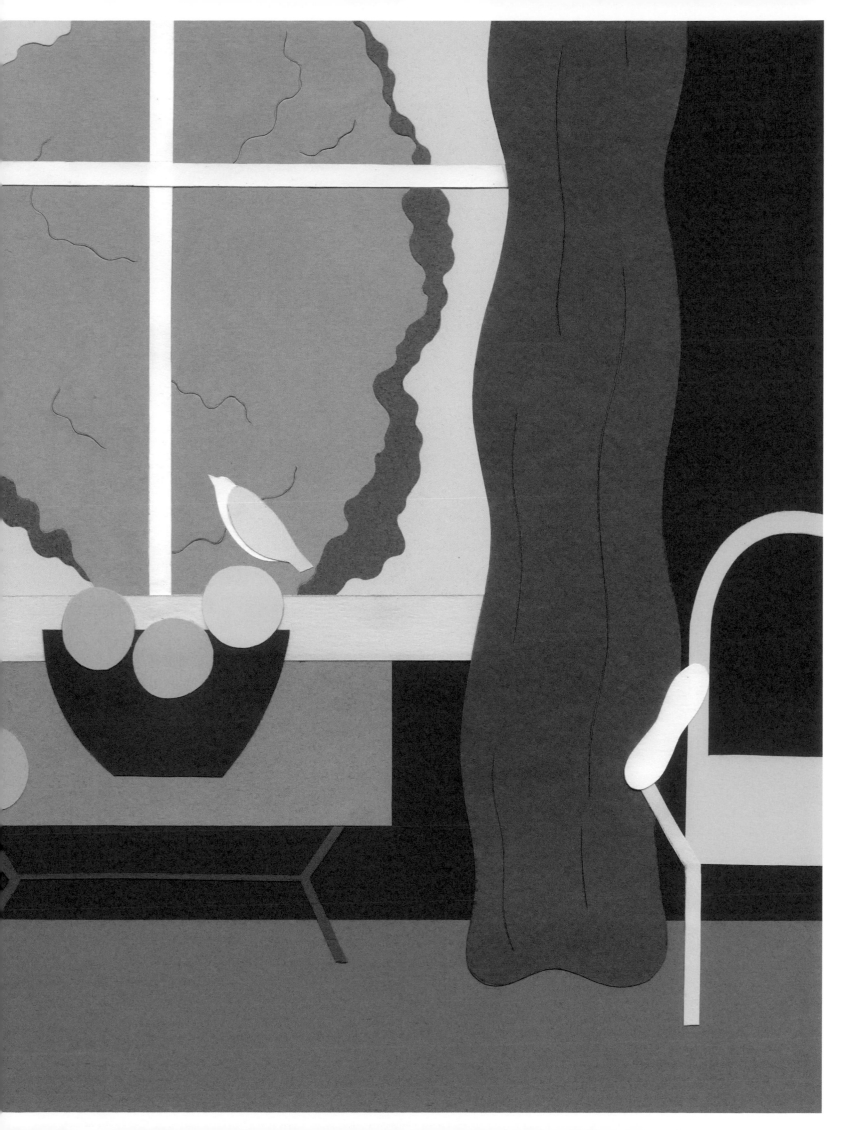

As he cut shape after shape from the white paper, he thought about a trip he had taken many years before, to the island of Tahiti. The shapes looked like the birds, fish, and seaweed he had seen there.

As his scissors glided through the paper, he thought about how a bird must feel when it flies. As he cut, Matisse felt like he, too, was flying.

Soon his walls were covered with plant and animal shapes. They captured the feeling of soaring and the sensation of swimming, but they didn't convey the bright blue of the sky or the deep blue of the sea.

So he made a new work, this time pinning his white forms to sheets painted azure and marine blue.

When he saw how the color brought his shapes to life, he asked his assistants to paint sheets of paper in a range of shades, from vermillion to lemon to violet. Instead of using only white paper, he decided he would make his shapes by cutting directly into color.

He tried a pink leaf against a background of orange, and a green leaf against a background of black. He cut leaves of other hues and set them against backgrounds of every shade, experimenting with different harmonies and contrasts—the way the colors played with and against each other.

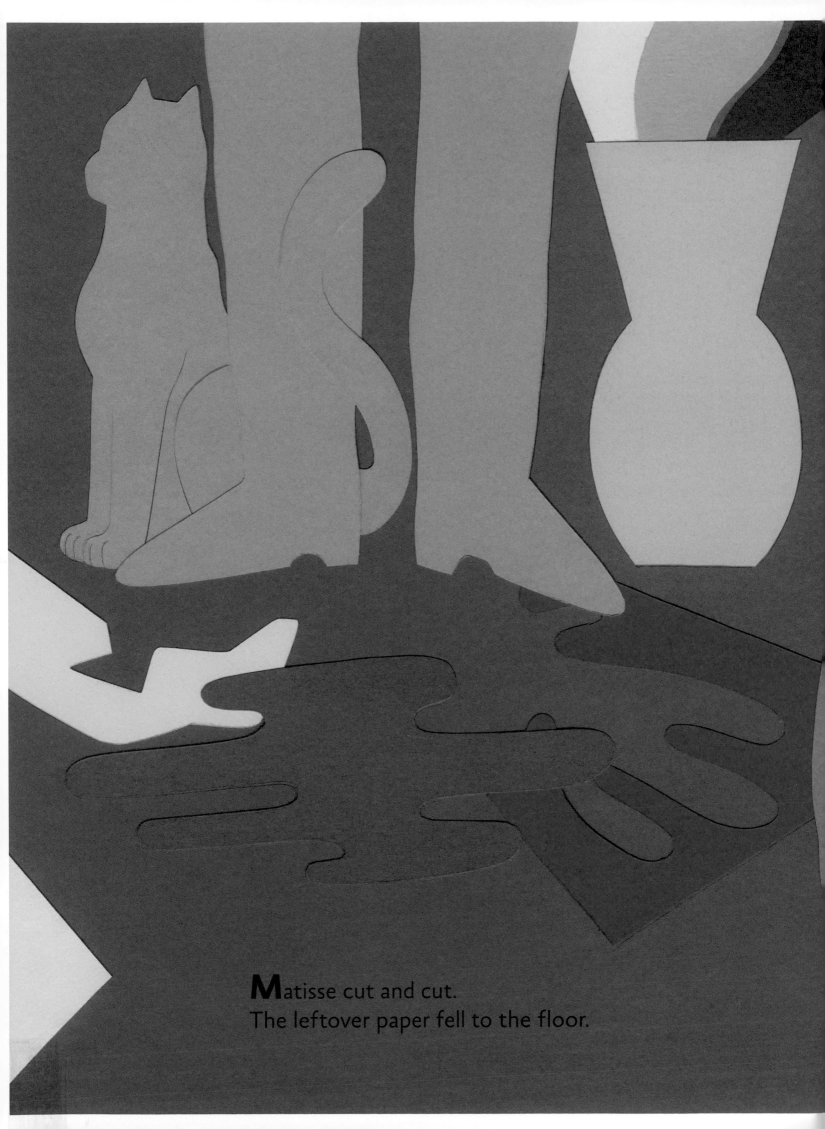

Matisse cut and cut.
The leftover paper fell to the floor.

"What counts most with colors are relationships," Matisse thought.

He realized that every shape he cut created another shape. Instead of throwing away the leftover pieces, he added them to the composition. They weren't leftovers at all!

H Matisse

Sometimes the shapes he cut were simple, like squares . . .

. . . but when he arranged them in just the
right way they took flight, like a swarm of bees.

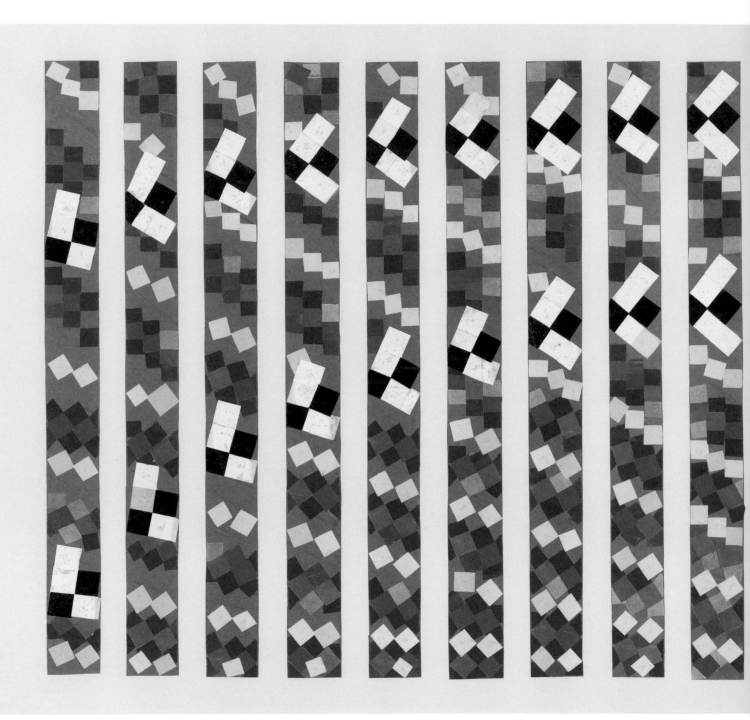

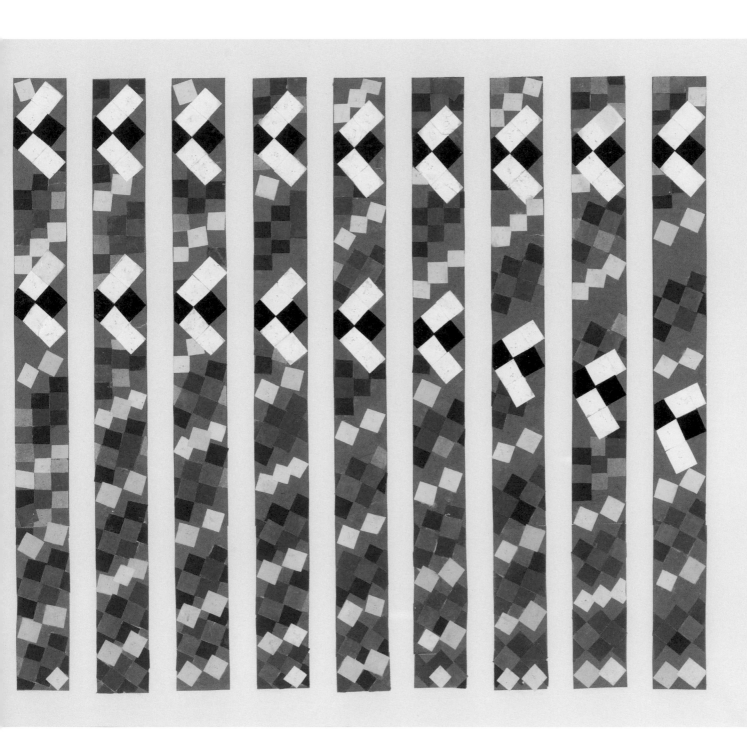

He composed his shapes to show
familiar scenes, like a woman
in a room with a vase of flowers . . .

. . . and he turned familiar objects into simple forms,
which he then composed into patterns.

His cut-outs started very small . . .

. . . and got larger . . .

. . . and then larger, as large as a wall! . . .

. . . until they stretched across the walls
of his studio, curving around corners
and covering doors.

Matisse realized happily, "I have made a little garden around me, where I can walk."

And for his garden, Matisse cut a small bird from a piece of blue paper.

Produced by the Department of Publications
The Museum of Modern Art, New York

Edited by Chul R. Kim and Emily Hall
Designed by Cristina Amodeo
Production by Hannah Kim
Printed and bound by Ofset Yapimevi, Istanbul

With thanks to Genevieve Allison, Karl Buchberg,
Madeleine Compagnon, Cerise Fontaine, Cari Frisch,
Jodi Hauptman, Elizabeth Margulies, Amanda Washburn,
Makiko Wholey, and Wendy Woon, and a special thanks
to Georges Matisse

This book is typeset in Absara Sans.
The paper is 150 gsm Amber Graphic.

Library of Congress Control Number: 2014939198
ISBN: 978-0-87070-910-4

Published by The Museum of Modern Art
11 West 53 Street
New York, New York 10019
www.moma.org

Distributed in the United States and Canada
by Abrams Books for Young Readers,
an imprint of ABRAMS, New York

Distributed outside the United States and Canada
by Thames & Hudson Ltd.

Printed in Turkey

PHOTOGRAPH CREDITS

HENRI MATISSE (1869–1954)

Henri Matisse was born in 1869, in Le Cateau-Cambrésis, in northern France. He trained to be a lawyer but took up painting while recovering from appendicitis. In 1891 he went to Paris to study art at the Académie Julian, and he became an apprentice to the painter Gustave Moreau. In the summers of 1904 and 1905, in the sunlit South of France, Matisse began to paint with bright, clashing colors. This style was eventually called Fauvism, after a critic called Matisse and other artists painting in this manner *fauves*, or wild beasts.

From there Matisse continued along a path he described as "construction by means of color." On a visit to Morocco in 1912 and 1913 he took in light, architecture, and textiles that influenced his painting; during his Nice period, from 1917 to 1930, he focused on female figures, interiors, and still lifes. In the 1930s and '40s Matisse turned increasingly to printmaking, and in the last decade of his life he pioneered a new form that came to be known as cut-outs, creating perhaps his most radical works at the end of his career. He died in 1954, at the age of eighty-four.

WORKS BY MATISSE

Polynesia, the Sky. 1946

Maquette for tapestry
Gouache on paper, cut and pasted, mounted on canvas
6′ 6 ¾″ x 10′ 3 ⁵/₈″ (200 x 314 cm)
Centre Pompidou, Paris. Musée national d'art moderne/Centre de création industrielle

Polynesia, the Sea. 1946

Maquette for tapestry
Gouache on paper, cut and pasted, mounted on canvas
6′ 5 ³/₁₆″ x 10′ 3 ⁵/₈″ (196 x 314 cm)
Centre Pompidou, Paris. Musée national d'art moderne/Centre de création industrielle

Composition (The Velvets). 1947

Gouache on paper, cut and pasted
20 ¼″ × 7′ 1 ⁵/₈″ (51.5 × 217.5 cm)
Kunstmuseum Basel. Acquired with support from
Dr. Richard Doetsch-Benziger, Basel, and Marguerite Hagenbach, Basel

Composition, Black and Red. 1947

Gouache on paper, cut and pasted
16 × 20 ¾″ (40.6 × 52.7 cm)
Davis Museum and Cultural Center, Wellesley College, Wellesley, Massachusetts. Gift of Professor and Mrs. John McAndrew

The Bees. Summer 1948

Preliminary maquette for the side windows
of the Chapel of the Rosary, Vence
Gouache on paper, cut and pasted, mounted on canvas
39 ¾″ × 7′ 10 ⁷/₈″ (101 × 241 cm)
Musée Matisse, Nice. Gift of the artist's family

Zulma. Early 1950

Gouache on paper, cut and pasted
7′ 9 ¹¹/₁₆″ × 52 ³/₈″ (238 × 133 cm)
Statens Museum for Kunst, Copenhagen

Chinese Fish. 1951

Maquette for stained-glass window
Gouache on paper, cut and pasted,
and charcoal on white paper, mounted on canvas
6′ 2 ¾″ × 35 ½″ (189.9 × 90.2 cm)
Colección Patricia Phelps de Cisneros

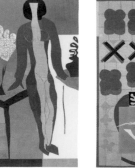

The Parakeet and the Mermaid. 1952

Gouache on paper, cut and pasted, and charcoal on white paper
11′ ⁵/₈″ × 25′ 2″ (337 × 768.5 cm)
Collection Stedelijk Museum, Amsterdam, acquired with the generous support of the Vereniging Rembrandt and the Prins Bernhard Cultuurfonds